*Let us preserve the memory of
the deserving: perhaps it may
prompt others likewise to deserve.*

DR. FOTHERGILL, 1763

QUAKER PROFILES

Pictorial and Biographical

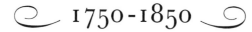 1750-1850

ANNA COX BRINTON

Pendle Hill Publications

Designed by Eleanore Price Mather

The type used is Baskerville monotype and linotype. The original face was cut by John Baskerville, distinguished printer of the eighteenth century, who experimented largely with papers, inks, and type founding. He was the personal friend of Dr. John Fothergill, one of the following "Profiles."

Printed in the United States of America
by Sowers Printing Company
Lebanon, Pennsylvania

November 1964: 3,000

Contents

Illustrations

Introduction

FRIENDS belonging to the first generation of Quakerism consistently refused to have their portraits drawn or painted. They preferred to be remembered by their deeds, preserved in their journals, in the meeting records, or prefixed to early Quaker publications which gathered up the facts of the lives of faithful members and perpetuated the love in which they were held. The pictures of George Fox and others which have come down to us from that age are of dubious authenticity.

Gradually the testimony against portraits relaxed. Simple likenesses in profile, especially shadow pictures, came to be countenanced. Because a shadow belongs to the natural world Friends had no objection to it. Light from the fireplace cast the "cat's dark silhouette on the wall" in Whittier's *Snow Bound,* just as Robert Louis Stevenson's "little shadow" from the nursery poem was produced by candle

1

light. Today bedtime candles and even fire-places are practically obsolete, but people continue to enjoy shadows, and finger-play is still practiced by grandparents to cheer reluctant children bound for bed on winter evenings.

So, as photography is now taken for granted as the major means of recording and transmitting the visible aspect of persons and events, a hundred years ago "the scissors art" was the economical and democratic method of taking likenesses, serving as a link between the modern photograph and the era of elaborate portraiture in oils of the rich and noble.

Basically the concept was not new. Profile portraits are as old as art. Men and animals seen from the side adorn the prehistoric caves in southern France; Egypt, Assyria, and Greece employed profiles as decorations, both monumental and minute. But the longest single series of profile heads appears on coins, for it was not many centuries after the introduction of metal disks as a medium of exchange that a human head was found to be a suitable ornament for them. These in turn left their impress on Italy during the Renaissance, when portrait medals of dignitaries had a long and honorable history and many great painters chose to portray their sitters in profile. To this already ancient tradition of portraiture belong the small wax or paper likenessess of the later eighteenth and early nineteenth centuries, which we know as the age of the silhouette.

The name is French, derived from Etienne de Silhouette, controller general of the finances of France in 1759, though as we use it the name was not applied until the following century. Because he was parsimonious, and perhaps also because he did paper cut-outs himself as a hobby, his name was given to these cheap representations. But the truth of the matter is that black shadow profiles were cut out years before Etienne de Silhouette. A certain Mrs. Pyburg, for example, cut profiles of the British royal couple, William and Mary, as early as 1699 and there is no reason to suppose that she initiated the method.

The Process

Essentially the process was simple. You placed your subject between a candle and a large sheet of paper and traced the shadow. The results were crude and unwieldy but the likeness was there. The procedure is still a pastime for children. But it developed into an art in the hands of portraitists who plied their skill in a variety of media which included modelling in wax, painting on glass, ivory, or paper, and, of course, paper-cutting.

And as an art paper-cutting is not dead yet. Even after a hundred years of photography deft profilists continue to appear at fairs, and in Asia paper-cutting is still practiced, being classed with jugglery as a popular amusement. I have seen a paper-cutter at a children's party in Japan dance while he clipped out elaborate scenes of daily life—persons walking in the rain carrying umbrellas, or drinking parties at wayside inns. *The New York Times* recently carried a statement to the effect that in the Soviet Union even shoeshine boys and silhouette cut-out artists are employees of the state. This shows that scissors work is still practiced, and that, simple art though it is, it serves as one more illustration of the transfer from private initiative to public regimentation.

Being easy and cheap to make, these paper likenesses found wide acceptance both in the world of fashion and within the Quaker fold. The plain dress proved a convenience to the cutter, because once a person had mastered the style he could use the same characteristic lines for other sitters. Men's tricorn and broad-brimmed hats and women's bonnets, caps and

Mary Richards

shawls were not difficult to cut. Sometimes the female costume was so all enveloping that it obviated the necessity of showing any features at all. Little Mary Richards, shown here, is so engulfed in her bonnet that we may never know what she looked like as an individual, but in a few simple lines her small figure catches the Empire period in which she lived, new-fangled umbrella and all.

Hollow Cut

This white-on-black portrait illustrates a variant from the more usual black-on-white style. The technique was called "hollow cut," the likeness being cut in white paper, leaving a hole to be backed with a dark fabric or other substance. This was a somewhat more difficult form of the art and for portrait heads was often aided by a machine.

The Peale Museum of Philadelphia, specializing in hollow cuts, used an instrument call-

4

ed a physiognotrace, invented in 1802. Its product at once became a fad. As an advertisement for the Museum sitters were allowed to operate the contraption themselves and for one cent—the cost of the paper—obtain a self-portrait. Now Charles Wilson Peale, the museum's head, had a mulatto slave whom he threatened to emancipate. This man, Moses Williams by name, was given charge of the physiognotrace and allowed to manipulate it for hesitant customers at a charge for his services of eight cents a cut. In the first year he produced almost nine thousand profiles.

So Moses Williams grew rich. He bought a house and then married the Peales' white cook. Such is the story in brief as told by Charles Coleman Sellers, the biographer of Peale.

Elaborations

In some cases these white figures were elab-

5

orated with a fine quill pen; black cuts show linear detail in white or gold. The pencil had been but recently invented, about 1750, and for sketching backgrounds proved far more practical than charcoal and chalk. These backgrounds were used increasingly as the technique developed to show groups as well as individuals. Group pictures had the great advantage of indicating relative size which a simple head and shoulders or a single figure standing alone could not. For example, we know from a contemporary municipal record that Stephen Grellet at the age of nineteen was five feet two inches and a half in height. Though he may have grown a little after that, it is unlikely that he attained average height, but his full-length silhouette does not in the least convey this shortness of stature. It was the groups or conversation pieces of the nineteenth century that inform us on relative height.

Because of this advantage in suggesting proportion and because of increased opportunities for characterization, the group picture was preferred by August Edouart, the most fashionable practitioner of the art. An exile from his native France after Napoleon's downfall, he failed as a French teacher before hitting his stride in 1825 as a silhouettist. He is said to have been the first to apply the name "silhouette" to the form. After great success in England he came to the United States as the recognized master of his craft, and for ten years toured the country doing individuals and groups, among them a number of Quaker families, two of which we include.

Close upon his heels in reputation and in time was the American, William Henry Brown, whose exquisite touch with the scissors and skill at characterization and composition approached the French master's. Brown was born 1808 in Charleston, South

Carolina, of Quaker parents. He died in 1883. A giant of a man, his energy was inexhaustible in portraying his fellow countrymen, including all the notable political figures of his age. But so far I have not found a Quaker in the lot. His speed was amazing. He took only one to five minutes to cut a figure, and sometimes he had finished before his sitter realized he had begun.

In return for this skill he received only a few cents a cut. Yet it was not his low rates that ended his career, but the explorations of two Frenchmen, Niepce and Daguerre, who applied the shadow in a new form. In 1859, as the Civil War was brewing, Brown acknowledged the triumph of the new era by giving up portraiture and going to work for the Huntington and Broadtop Railroad. Daguerre's camera had won; the daguerreotype took the place of the silhouette as the popular medium for portraiture.

The Amateur Cutter

While the professionals were recording the personalities of their age for a livelihood, the amateurs were wielding their scissors, too, led by Queen Charlotte, the wife of the ill-fated George III. As men and women today turn to art as a means of self expression, amusement, therapy, and to pass the time, so in that age they took up paper-cutting—aided and abetted by the importation of the pencil from Germany, the manufacture of scissors, the cheapness of paper, and increasing leisure.

And in this fashion the world of the court and the world of Quakerism were at one. Thomas Clarkson in his once famous book, *A Portraiture of Quakerism,* says quite simply, "Quakers are a happy people." This he attributes to their care of one another, their comfortable circumstances, their attachment to family life, and their avoidance of idleness.

Congenial association and improving entertainment banished the temptation to kill time among Quaker girls, who often studied the same lessons as their brothers. Among the diversions permitted to these religiously centered people who disapproved of cards, dancing, theatre, and the hunt were amateur  science, guessing games, needlework, and—papercutting.

The results of their creativity were incorporated in albums. I have myself seen in England a huge album, larger than an "elephant folio" filled with lifesized shadow portraits of several generations of the Robson family. Having been held together by a substantial cover, the individual likenesses have not disintegrated, as usually occurs with big profiles, which are seldom preserved intact. And in the neighborhood of Philadelphia I know of two albums that have survived: a book of Comly family portraits belonging to Helen Comly Bacon of Wallingford, Pennsylvania, and an older and smaller album now in the library of the Pennsylvania Historical Society. This was made in 1792 by Joseph Sansom, brother of William Sansom (see page 35). It consists of inked drawings, "intended," as he states in his preface, "as a memorial of particular friends and remarkable contemporaries." In regard to the likenesses he says it was the first stroke that conveyed the resemblance, and he warned against retouching. With scissors work, of course, the question of retouching seldom, if ever, arose.

There are also many examples of the art which have survived without benefit of the safety and seclusion of an album. In the Evans family a beautiful series of unmounted profiles, a number of them from that extraordinary Philadelphia institution, the Peale Museum, has been preserved in good condition.

These collections reflect a fraction of the people, animals, and natural objects which were cut, drawn, or inked in uncounted numbers all through the colonial period and up to the invention of photography. Because the materials involved were fragile comparatively few have come down to us. But these few, along with samplers and needlework maps, are treasured by descendants of the deft artificers who made them, or are collected and preserved by museums, libraries, and historical societies. Many are unidentified, and we all know how tantalizing it is to inherit an album or box of unnamed likenesses. But many others we know by name, and thanks to this art process we have at least heads and busts of most of the leading Friends of that time.

The Present Album

This pamphlet is a diminutive album presenting a portraiture of selected members of the Society of Friends between 1750 and 1850. These include heads, full length figures, and groups. In some cases the cutters are known; others are anonymous. The full length figures and groups are most often cut by professionals. But whether wrought by a professional or an amateur, these portraits illustrate the period when Quakers were most clearly distinguished from others by their speech, dress, and behavior. In speech, this meant the singular pronoun instead of the honorific "you" to one person, whether prince or pauper; in dress, adherence to an inherited style without change to conform to fashion; in behavior, omission of the accepted modes of showing deference to superiors. Neither before King nor Pope would they bow or uncover their heads. Most of us know the story of William Penn, hat on head before King Charles II. The King removed his own hat, and when Penn asked, "Friend Charles, wherefore dost thou uncover thyself?" the King replied with a smile, "Friend Penn, it is the custom of this place for only one man to wear his hat at a time!" In the case of Stephen Grellet, Vatican officials acted firmly but with finesse when the interpreting priest led the Quaker into the Pope's apartment. "As I was entering the door," wrote Stephen Grellet, "someone behind me gently, but quickly, took off my hat, and before I could look for it, the door was quietly closed upon us three."

The scruples of these Friends in respect to equality may sometimes appear to us to be strained, but we are not through wrestling with the basic problem of treating all men as equals, of avoiding superfluity in dress, house, and table, and of achieving manners at once respectful and democratic. As we look at their plain garb in the silhouettes it has a certain attractiveness, reminding us of a generation that had, perhaps, a greater faithfulness than our own.

There are several ways of looking at these Quaker profiles. One is to view them simply as items of decoration where neither subject nor artist is of special interest in itself. Another is as family documentary items in which the name and date of the person or persons represented is the important point. A third is to consider authorship: can we tell who cut the likeness, was he or she professional or amateur, when and where did the artist live and work? Finally, and this is the factor of which I have taken special account: what aspect of the experience and work of the Society of Friends does the subject of this profile illustrate?

Dr. John Fothergill　1712-1780

A S A DOCTOR, a botanist, and a philanthropist Dr. Fothergill represents the quintessence of Quakerism. He was eminent in the medical profession, helping his brother physicians to pass from the old authoritarian rules for bleeding and blistering to a treatment relying on building up the patient's strength so as to enable him to resist disease. A keen clinical observer, careful to record and publish his observations, he was a pioneer in overcoming smallpox by inoculation. It was he who selected an English physician to inoculate Catharine the Great of Russia and her son the Grand Duke, who was heir to the throne. As the latter was a frail youth the enterprise was fraught with peril—so much so that the Empress made special arrangement for the doctor and his party to be spirited out of the country in case anything should go wrong!

Dr. Fothergill was also an enthusiastic botanist and general scientist who imported from abroad plants unknown before in England. He wrote the preface to his friend Dr. Benjamin Franklin's "Letters on Electricity," and sponsored Joseph Priestley's chemical researches. Though Friends of this period considered pictures a superfluity he was strongly impressed with their educational value. To the Pennsylvania Hospital he presented a series of anatomical drawings still to be seen there.

As philanthropist he worked to put an end to the slave trade and free the slaves; to reform prisons and give productive work to prisoners; to resuscitate persons from drowning and suffocation; and to establish a national system of vital statistics, a project not realized till after his death. The first census in Great Britain was taken in 1801 and the registration of births, deaths, and marriages was not regularized until 1837. Dr. Fothergill also spent a great deal of effort on city planning for London, though its streets—in spite of his best efforts—remained crooked in the region around St. Paul's Cathedral until after World War II.

Food for the people in time of war and famine was much on Fothergill's mind as it was on the minds of all the leading Friends of this period, and he insisted that medical care was of little use for underfed patients. To London bakers he circulated a recipe for augmenting the scarce wheat flour with potato in their bread.

But it is with John Fothergill, Quaker, that we are mainly concerned here. He was from childhood a consistent Friend, unlike his younger brother, Samuel (1715-1772), the great preacher, a youth so wayward that his father, setting out in the love of Truth on his third visit to America, said to him, "And now, son Samuel, farewell; farewell; and unless it be as a changed man, I can not say that I have any wish ever to see thee again." Samuel went through a crisis, and with his friends' help "turned the current of a highly gifted life into the ways of truth." When the father returned in 1738 he came late into a meeting at York, where he stood up and spoke. Presently he stopped, saying that what he had to impart "was given to another." A young Friend followed with a powerful sermon. Not till the elder Fothergill inquired afterwards who it was did he realize that it was his son Samuel who had completed his message.

By thrift, industry, and honesty, Quakers after three generations, had acquired wealth and faced a new problem. Dr. Fothergill devoted himself heart and soul to revitalizing the essential principles of the Society of Friends. Unlike his father and brother he was an elder rather than a minister. Three times he served as Clerk of London Yearly Meeting. His hope was in restoration of the discipline, and to this end he sought a better standard of education than was characteristic of Friends in general at that time. To encourage reading, Fothergill took a major part in the publication of Baskerville's handsome edition of Barclay's *Apology,* and he and his brother Samuel drew up the account of Quakerism for the first edition of the *Encyclopedia Britannica* in 1768. He also wrote the preface for the giant folio of 1771, *Selected Works of William Penn.*

For Friends in moderate and less than moderate circumstances Ackworth School was opened in 1779 as a result of his unremitting efforts. While Dr. Fothergill moved among all classes and took part in the best intellectual life of his day, he was exact in maintaining Friends' habits and testimonies, even their peculiarities in speech, dress, and manners. He could not become a physician to the King because this would have required his taking the Oath of Allegiance.

The Society of Friends in England and America was at this time one society, interpenetrated by the visits of travelling ministers, two of whom were Fothergills, the doctor's father and brother. Scientific interest also united Friends across the Atlantic. More fully informed regarding the colonies than most of his countrymen, Dr. Fothergill was active in the role of conciliator. In cooperation with his friend, Dr. Benjamin Franklin, he tried his utmost to reconcile the colonies with the parent government. The effort failed, but all through the war Fothergill and his friends endeavored to keep channels of communication open till at last everything was yielded by the British except independence. But it was too late. Shortly before his death in 1780

Fothergill wrote to Franklin, then in Paris, "Much horrible mischief would have been prevented had our superiors thought fit to pay any regard to our humble endeavors. But their ears were shut, their hearts hardened, . . ." When informed of Dr. Fothergill's death a few weeks later, Franklin said, "I think a worthier man never lived."

To a nephew we owe the following minute account of the doctor's appearance:

"He usually wore a large low three-cornered hat; a white medical wig, with rows of small curls descending one under another from near the crown to his shoulders; a coat, waistcoat and breeches of nearly white superfine cloth; the coat without any collar, large cuffs, and two of the buttons buttoned over his breast; the waistcoat with long flaps; the ends of his cravat were buttoned within his waistcoat; the stockings he wore were silk and the colour of his clothes; his buckles were small."

Our medallion of Dr. Fothergill bears out this description. It is said to have been designed by Patience Lovell Wright, daughter of Quaker parents in Bordentown, New Jersey. From childhood she had a bent for portraiture, modelling profiles from putty, dough, candle ends—any malleable material that came to hand. Early left a widow with small children, she went to London in 1772 where her work immediately became fashionable.

She was employed from time to time by Josiah Wedgewood, one of Dr. Fothergill's correspondents. It was for him that she designed this profile.

Her son Joseph, whom she took to England as a little boy, grew up to be an artist. Before the War of Separation he returned to America, where he painted portraits and it was he who designed the first United States currency.

Rebecca Jones   1739-1818

AMONG FRIENDS in America the most widely known woman Minister of the Gospel—or "M.G." as we often find noted on the silhouettes—was Rebecca Jones. Also the best beloved, she is one of the few Quaker women included in the forthcoming biographical dictionary of *Notable American Women, 1607-1950,* sponsored by Radcliffe College.

She was born in Philadelphia July 8, 1739. After the death of her father her widowed mother, a loyal member of the Church of England, carried on a successful school for little girls in her home in Drinkers Alley. It was her ambition to fit Rebecca to become a distinguished teacher, but she did not live long enough to realize how well she had succeeded.

As a child "romping Beck Jones" often attended Friends meetings with her playmates. The silence appealed to her but she "liked not" the Quaker way of preaching, perhaps referring to the chanting intonation then current. Eventually her mother realized that this influence was striking deeper than she had expected. Determining to thwart it, she called on Rebecca's elder brother, Daniel, to exert his influence. He inquired, "Is she not dutiful?" to which the mother answered,

"More dutiful than before." The brother's advice was, "Leave her alone."

Meanwhile Rebecca was going through an intense inner struggle to surrender her own will to Divine Guidance. Worn to a shadow by this struggle, she sank into a depression from which she was rescued by Catherine Peyton, a visiting English Friend, toward whom she felt a lifelong gratitude. At the age of nineteen she took the momentous step of speaking in a Friends' meeting for worship, and before two years were up her gift in the ministry was recorded by her monthly meeting. There was now no doubt that she had thrown in her lot with the Quakers.

Soon after this her mother died and the school devolved upon Rebecca, who carried it on for more than twenty years. She never married. Her pupils loved and respected her, their parents had confidence in her. John Woolman was one of her devoted friends.

Mottoes for her pupils' writing lessons inscribed by his skillful pen are still to be seen in the library of Haverford College. Rebecca Jones often spent her vacations at Mount Holly, dividing the time between her brother Daniel, a warden of St. Andrews Church, who kept an inn there, and John and Sarah Woolman.

She was also much at home with the Allinson family in Burlington, New Jersey. On one occasion their little son, having been naughty, was sent to bed without supper. Next morning he came down radiant, as children often do after punishment. Rebecca Jones said sternly, "But I have not forgot thy conduct of last evening." Quick as a flash he answered with a stanza from Watts:

> "The wise will let their anger cool
> At least before 'tis night,
> But in the bosom of a fool
> It lasts till morning light."

She had met her match! This little boy grew up to be her biographer.

At the age of forty-five, when she was at the height of her powers, handsome and blessed with easy and gracious manners, she gave up her teaching and laid before her Monthly Meeting a concern to visit Friends in England. Credentials were granted by the Monthly, Quarterly, and Yearly Meetings, and with six other Friends, "all intending for Great Britain," she sailed from Newcastle, Delaware. The captain later remarked in a London coffee house that he had "brought over an American Quaker lady who possessed more sense than both Houses of Parliament." During her stay of four years she attended 1,578 meetings for worship and discipline, and 1,120 meetings with Friends in the station of servants, apprentices, and laborers. In an uncounted number of religious visits to families she appeared under a sense of "fresh and sure direction," which was constantly renewed.

It was Sarah Hustler, daughter of Christiana Hustler, intimate friend and companion in the ministry of Rebecca Jones, who drew, reduced, and cut the accompanying profile, which represents the shadow portrait in its simplest form. It was made while Rebecca Jones was staying at the hospitable home of the Hustler family near Bradford in Yorkshire, a favorite rendezvous for travelling ministers from across the ocean. The father, John Hustler, a wool stapler and minister among Friends, worked with Dr. Fothergill to make more food, especially fish, available to the poor in times of scarcity.

In 1793 Rebecca Jones succumbed to the yellow fever epidemic which depopulated Philadelphia of more than 4,000 inhabitants. Her life was despaired of. At one moment the nurse, to ease her demise, was about to withdraw her pillow, when the young attending physician intervened. "No, no," said he, "I can't let her die." Himself assuming the duties of nurse, he tended her through the night and by morning she began to mend. To Thomas Scattergood, who visited her daily, sometimes oftener, we owe a vivid account of this experience.

She lived to resume her ministry among Friends, not only of Philadelphia, but of New York and New England as well, and to take up the wide correspondence which was a major activity of her later years. Her style of writing is stately, never hasty or careless, though often repetitious, as is not unnatural in letter writing. Its tone of self-abnegation was less her own than a mannerism of the time. Original words, phrases, and even wit enliven many of her letters. She had several striking premonitions, and of these she says, "The Lord has in some instances entrusted me with his secrets, and I have not betrayed them." No wonder she was much confided in.

Late in her career Rebecca Jones contributed her knowledge of Friend's education in England, where she had more than once visited Ackworth School, to the founding of Westtown School. Nor did she lack the practical touch. At the time of its opening, when at the last minute a supply of dishes was urgently needed, she is said to have originated the idea of collecting the pewter then being replaced by china in the homes of well-to-do Friends. Plates, platters, and porringers were brought to her door in wheelbarrow loads for shipment by wagon to the school. It was not until 1803 that she herself first visited Westtown. The girls, she wrote, "are preciously promising."

For more than fifty years she was a trusted advisor and informal almoner of many Friends. Her eyes and her heart were open for the poor and oppressed and others in critical need. The most exciting episode in her memoirs is her achievement of the rescue of a beautiful girl, an ex-slave, abducted in a ship already under way for the West Indies. She was a frequent visitor at that quaint establishment, the Friends' Almshouses, and her will included a special legacy for poor Friends of

her own meeting. Even in extreme old age her advice was sought on important occasions. "Here sits our Queen," cheerfully exclaimed her old friend Thomas Scattergood in 1814, when he called upon her the last time he left his own house before he died.

In the Minutes of Philadelphia Monthly Meeting for the Northern District the fact is recorded that Rebecca Jones died on the fifteenth of the Fourth Month, 1818, in the 79th year of her age—"in peace and unity with his (Christ's) church under every name," as she had written in her will. She was buried in the Friends' ground on Mulberry (now Arch) Street on the morning of the Yearly Meeting of Ministers and Elders, the Friends passing from her grave into the meeting house with minds solemnized by the remembrance of this beloved fellow member who had so often caused them to feel the Divine authority which rested upon her.

Nicholas Waln   1742-1813

NICHOLAS WALN is remembered by most Quakers of today for his wit, a gift particularly prized in the Society of Friends. But in his own time he was venerated as a "Public Friend"—meaning one who appeared in the ministry—who had had the courage to give up a cherished career as a lawyer for the sake of religious duty.

Born at Fairhill and educated in Philadelphia, he was already well grounded in literature and mathematics when he took to the law and studied both in Philadelphia and London. Significantly, he also made himself fluent in the German language, for the rich farmlands of Lancaster County were by this time populated with German-speaking farmers, drawn to the New World by Penn's hospitality to Rheinlanders, who appreciated a lawyer with whom they could freely communicate in their own language. With them and with many others Nicholas Waln established a lucrative practice.

At the height of his affluence he remarked of a colleague that this man "was not roguish enough for a lawyer." That was a straw indicating which way the wind was turning. For about this time on the way home from Newtown, where the courts for Bucks County were then held, Nicholas stopped in to see a friend, and speaking of the recent sessions told him, "I did the best I could for my client, gained the case for him, and thereby defrauded an honest man out of his just due."

Not long after, overwhelmed by the "power of constraining grace," Nicholas Waln became "utterly disqualified for attending to business." Then came what he afterwards called the "judgment day." He went to the "Youths' Meeting" on the third day of the week at the Market Street Meeting House, and here delivered a prayer concerning his own condition which produced a remarkable effect not only upon his friends, but on the citizens generally. Various attempts were made to write it down from memory, but the versions did not completely agree. However the general purport was this:

"Oh Lord God . . . Wash me in the laver of regeneration. Thou hast done much for me, and hast a right to expect much;—therefore, in the presence of this congregation, I resign myself and all that I have, to thee, O Lord!—it is thine; and I pray thee, O Lord! to give me grace to enable me to continue in this resolution!"

When the Meeting closed Nicholas Waln hurried home and immediately fell ill. A month later William Logan of Philadelphia wrote to Samuel Clarke of London:

"It may be new to thee, perhaps, to be informed, that thy friend, my relation, Nicholas Waln, has, from being almost at the head of the law with us, in high esteem and great practice, from a very sudden and unexpected change, left the calling, and is likely to become a Public Friend . . . If he is rightly called . . . I make no doubt of his being as serviceable in the gallery, and in the Society, as at the bar."

For several years Nicholas lived a retired life, but was diligent in attending meetings, at first seldom appearing as a minister. A decade later he spent two years visiting the meetings of Friends in England, and ten years after that traveled in Ireland, a preacher admired alike by Friends and others. Then came another change. His communications during the last fifteen years of his life were "generally in a few words, but weighty and adapted to particular states."

In business meetings, where his legal and financial experience would seem to have justified active participation, he kept in the background and when a decision was reached he seemed rather to follow than to make any feel that he had led them. He was a reconciler who in differences of opinion advocated patience and "keeping low," as he says, so as to unite with the judgment of Truth.

He was an overseer of the twelve or more public schools founded by Penn's charter in the town and county of Philadelphia; most of these were for boys but a few were for "female children." Though his own special interest was in the Latin schools, he was a

diligent visitor to all the schools. The countenances of the pupils would brighten when they saw him coming. Sometimes he preached to the children in such simple and impressive words that after they had grown up many of them remembered what he had said.

We are glad to observe that giving up professional ambition and delight in riches did not deprive him of his sense of fun or zest for people. We conclude this sketch with a whimsical touch characteristic of the many anecdotes about Nicholas Waln:

A woman Friend, a minister, was subject to fits of depression. Nicholas calling one day to see her, she began, "Nicholas, I am going to die." "I think there is no doubt but thou will," said he, "and when thou gets to heaven give my love to the Apostle Paul, and tell him I wish he would come back to earth and explain some of the hard things in his Epistles."

The silhouette on page 23 cut by Mary Hanor catches him in just such a moment, one finger raised in kindly admonishment as he prods his friend out of despair by setting her to think about something beside herself.

Paul Cuffe   1759-1817

CAPTAIN PAUL CUFFE (pronounced and often spelled Cuffee), was a native of New England, son of a freed slave who was an attender of Friends Meeting. At the age of sixteen he took to the sea on a whaling expedition to the Gulf of Mexico. His second voyage as a common seaman was to the West Indies. On his third, during the Revolutionary War, he was captured by the British and detained for three months in New York.

The lure of the sea was dimmed by this captivity and when he was released he went home to farm and family. Here he devoted his spare time to study, concentrating on arithmetic and navigation. Of the latter he says, "Lesson I, all as black as midnight. Lesson II, a little gleam of light. Lesson III, more light." "There were always three things," he continued, "to which I paid attention—latitude, lead, lookout." With his brother, David, he built an open boat for coastwise traffic. Pirates attacked, and cargo and boat were lost. A second venture fared no better, and on a third trip headed for Nantucket his cargo was pillaged by pirates. But his next two voyages were whaling expeditions to Newfoundland which brought adequate financial returns, and at the age of thirty-six he was

PAUL

CAPTAIN

CUFFEE

1812.

*This likeness of Paul Cuffe
was made in Bristol, England.
His ship "The Traveller"
was doubtless drawn from
life. The shore scene of
Sierra Leone may well
have been designed from
a verbal description.*

26

master of a schooner of sixty-nine tons burden. Captain Cuffe's voyages extended from Eastern ports of the United States to the West Indies, England, Russia, and Africa.

William J. Allinson writes in a memoir of Paul Cuffe, ". . . although naturally placed in obscurity with peculiar barriers in his way to distinction . . . he made his way onward and upward . . . by the mere force of individual worth." Paul Cuffe became a member of the Society of Friends and early contributed to the erection of a new meetinghouse. I am indebted to Thomas E. Drake for the comment that "he preached seldom but when he did, with moving power."

The following anecdote is quoted by Henry J. Cadbury in an intensely interesting article in the *Journal of Negro History,* vol. xxi, 1936, "Negro Membership in the Society of Friends:" In shipping in and out of Norfolk harbor, Virginia, with his ship, Negro crew and cargo, he was quite unjustly refused clearance by the collector of the port because he was a Negro. He repaired for redress to Washington and when brought into President Madison's presence he declared, "James, I have been put to much trouble, and have been abused . . . I have come here for thy protection and have to ask thee to order thy Collector for the port of Norfolk to clear me out for New Bedford, Massachusetts." The request was immediately granted. President Madison's wife, Dolly, grew up a Friend in Philadelphia, so the President was no doubt familiar with the Quaker mode of address.

In middle life he developed a concern for American Negroes who were being repatriated to Africa. Advised by James Pemberton to seek consultation with Friends on the matter, Paul Cuffe laid his concern first before his fellow members in Westport, Massachusetts, then before Friends in Philadelphia. With

27

their encouragement he prepared at his own expense for his first voyage to Africa. His destination was Sierra Leone. But after examining conditions there he decided to return to Philadelphia, sailing by way of England. There, though he had trouble with a pressgang that took two of his sailors and sequestered a third, a young African who was apprenticed to him to learn navigation, he had a rewarding experience. He was gratified to discover a lively interest among English Friends, who were already considering a settlement in Sierra Leone. They found in him an unexpected ally, admirably suited for the work at hand. Tall, heavy set, and of "noble bearing," he combined prudence with resolution. And what is perhaps more surprising, considering the rugged nautical tradition of the times, his crew behaved with "conciliatory propriety." All in all this seemed a godsend.

The enterprise brought him into contact with several leading Friends, including William Allen, scientist, educator and philanthropist, companion of Stephen Grellet on his European travels, and Edward Pease, the "father of English railways." Captain Cuffe kept a diary of his stay in England which is now with his other papers in the New Bedford Library. It is the kind of record from which the Quaker Journals were written, but with a wealth of practical detail which we do not always find in this type of literature. Here he gives us a day by day account of trips to the Admiralty to obtain release of his men, business errands having to do with cargo and registration of the ship, sightseeing, including the East India docks, Friends visited, meetings attended, occasions on which he appeared in the ministry or in supplication.

Stephen Grellet in his Journal (1811) made this comment on Paul Cuffe's relations with Friends in England: "It has I believe opened the minds of many in tender feelings toward the poor suffering Africans who they see are men like themselves, capable of becoming like Paul Cuffe, valuable and useful members of civil and religious society." And William Allen hoped that, ". . . the present opportunity for promoting the civilization of Africa through the means of Paul Cuffe should not be lost: he seems like a man made on purpose for the business. . . ."

But the captain's American Indian wife was not willing to go to Africa and he would not press the matter. He told his English correspondents he would do all in his power to help the cause and would make occasional voyages. He set about organizing committees in Baltimore, Philadelphia, and New York to communicate with the African Institute in London and the Friendly Society of Sierra Leone. But these committees had no concern with trade, whereas Cuffe desired a sound economic basis for the community, or—to quote the old style cumbrous title: "A Society for the Purpose of Encouraging the Black Settlers at Sierra Leone, and the natives of Africa Generally in the Cultivation of their Soil, by the Sale of their Produce." Commerce could, he thought, become the neutral force linking together England, Africa, and the United States.

To all these efforts the War of 1812 and subsequent tensions presented an insurmountable obstruction.

Paul Cuffe died in 1817 at the age of fifty-nine. By his adventurous and diligent life he had amassed what was in those days a modest fortune. He knew how to save. To one of the many people who asked for his advice he wrote, "By experience I have ever found when I attended to my business I seldom suffered loss. I have found it to be good to make choice of good companions. I have ever found it not to be profitable for me to sit long after dining and make a tipling habit of wine and other liquors. These very people who adopt those practices when they see a sober steady man will put business in his way; the surest way to conquer strong drink is to make no use of it."

Societies that were by this time springing up to repatriate Negroes to Africa considered Paul Cuffe their pioneer. But it was in the mastery of poverty that he saw the solution of the problem of democracy. Perhaps we are today coming to agree with this conviction.

Hester Savory
1777-1803

WERE IT NOT for Charles Lamb the portrait above might be one of the hundreds of profiles that have come down to us unnamed. And if Hester had not been a Quaker, Charles Lamb's life-long predilection for the Society of Friends might have been less glowing.

The facts about her life are few, and are best told by Lamb himself in a letter to his friend, Thomas Manning, in March, 1803.

Dear Manning,

"I send you some verses I have made on the death of a young Quaker you may have heard me speak of as being in love with for some years while I lived at Pentonville, though I had never spoken to her in my life. She died about a month since. The young Quaker was Hester Savory, daughter of Joseph Savory, a goldsmith of the Strand. She married the 1st of July, 1802, and died a few months after."

That is all. We may read between the lines if we will, but there is little in actual fact beyond Lamb's statement, and this silhouette, which was made by John Field of London. Field was an ingenious artist who employed various media: paper and scissors, India ink on glass, paint on paper, sometimes enhanced with pencilled touches of gold, as in the present instance. Perhaps this use of gold was a reflection of his double calling, for he belonged to the firm of "Miers and Field, Profile Painters and Jewellers." As Hester's father, Joseph Savory, was a goldsmith he and Field may perhaps have known each other.

All his life Charles Lamb had close associations with the Quakers, first with Charles Lloyd and his children in Birmingham, later with Bernard Barton, the Quaker poet, unread today but a favorite with his own generation. In a letter to Coleridge in 1797 Lamb wrote: "Tell Lloyd I have had thoughts of turning Quaker, and have been reading, or am rather just beginning to read, a most capital book, good thoughts in good language, William Penn's *No Cross, No Crown*. I like it immensely."

Twenty-four years later Lamb published in the *London Magazine,* among his "Essays of Elia," the four pages entitled "A Quaker's Meeting," which begins:

"Reader, would'st thou know what true peace and quiet mean: would'st thou find a refuge from the noises and clamours of the multitude: would'st thou enjoy at once solitude and society; would'st thou possess the depth of thy own spirit in stillness, without being shut out from the consolatory faces of thy species; would'st thou be alone, and yet accompanied; solitary, yet not desolate; singular, yet not without some to keep thee in countenance; a unit in aggregate; a simple in composite: come with me into a Quaker's Meeting."

It is in this essay that the famous sentence occurs: "Get the writings of John Woolman by heart and love the early Quakers." But somewhat more critically he continues, "How far the followers of these good men in our days have kept to the primitive spirit, or in what proportion they have substituted formality for it, the Judge of Spirits can alone determine."

The verses which Lamb sent to Manning were not distinguished; some of us would consider them purely sentimental. Charles Lamb's real poetry was his prose. And his lasting tribute to Hester was not the elegy he wrote at the time of her death but the words in *Elia* written so many years later:

"Every Quakeress is a lily; and when they come up in bands to their Whitsun-conferences, whitening the easterly streets of the metropolis, from all parts of the United Kingdom, they show like troops of the Shining Ones."

Susanna Sansom   1766-1845

W E PRESENT Susanna Sansom after Hester Savory, because, though she was born eleven years before Hester, she survived the younger girl by more than forty years. Her long, full life as a wife and mother carried her into the mid-nineteenth century and into the spirit of a new age, which is indicated in the accompanying picture.

We see her here as the widow of an active Friend, William Sansom, 1763-1840. Earliest in the long line of real estate "developers" in Philadelphia, he, along with two or three others, took over at the sheriff's sale a great mansion which the French architect, Major L'Enfant, was erecting for Robert Morris, 1734-1806. Popularly called "Morris's Folly," it was referred to by its original owner as "a much more magnificent house than I ever intended to have built." It will be remembered that Robert Morris was the financier of the Revolutionary War, who pledged his private fortune to obtain supplies for the army when his personal credit was sounder than that of the new-fledged government. But his affairs became over-extended and the great financial house with which he was involved in Holland failed. Though Morris owned a large part of the land on which Washington now stands, the city did not build up as rapidly as was hoped and expected. Unable to meet the demands of his creditors Robert Morris was for three years imprisoned for debt, the bankruptcy law not being passed until 1800. After his release he lived in an unostentatious manner in a house on Twelfth Street.

A note in William Sansom's own hand states that he erected on the Morris premises eighty fine dwellings. These were the first row houses in a city which came to be famous for its red brick, marble stepped house fronts. For this project Sansom Street was cut through what had earlier been a pasture extending from High Street (now Market) to Walnut Street between Seventh and Eighth. The whole story as narrated in Watson's curious scrap book entitled *Annals of Philadelphia* and in more recent biographical material on Robert Morris is extremely complex and interesting.

Eliza Sansom Vaux, the daughter shown facing her mother in our illustration, was the wife of George Vaux, 1780-1836, to whom she was married in 1808. Another handsome silhouette cut by Edouart in the same year shows Eliza seated, surrounded by her children, two sons and seven daughters, all standing. These two cuttings remain in the Vaux family.

The present composition, cut in 1843 by August Edouart, repays careful scrutiny. On the table there is an album of silhouettes which Susanna Sansom may well have been examining, and she holds in her hand a pair of spectacles with the short earpieces of the period. These details must have been very difficult to cut—likewise the letter closed with sealing wax which is held by the servant, Philip Gurney, who is obviously caught at the moment of bringing in the mail.

Edouart informs us that he took with him on his travels from place to place lithograph backgrounds made in Ireland, also glass and frames. The backgrounds were to expedite his process, the glass and frames of yellow maple edged with black to make sure that his work should appear to the best advantage when mounted, because, as he wryly comments, his customers used such inappropriate materials for framing. The work illustrated here is enclosed in its original frame.

The room and its draperies are in the grand style of the mid-nineteenth century, and no doubt represent one of the readymade backgrounds which were part of the artist's equipment. They appear incongruous with the Quaker costume and Susanna Sansom's rocking chair. Fortunately this device sometimes gave way to spontaneous realism, as in our frontispiece, also probably by Edouart, which depicts the New York family of Abraham Underhill in their country home on the Eastern shore of Maryland. Here the background has been especially drawn for the occasion, showing windows with plain Venetian blinds, and the kind of furniture which Friends today appreciate inheriting as "antiques." The room and everything in it appeared, when I saw it a few years ago, exactly as Edouart has drawn it.

The Parrishes:

THE YEAR 1842-3 found August Edouart active in Philadelphia. The present illustration shows a scene dear to Dr. Joseph Parrish: his presentation eight years earlier, of the certificate of membership in the College of Physicians to his son, Isaac.

Joseph Parrish was born in 1779, youngest of eleven children. In the yellow fever scourge of 1793, two of his brothers perished. This induced in young Joseph, then 14, serious religious thoughts. It may also have predisposed him to the career of a physician. He studied medicine, and as a young doctor in his middle twenties was selected by the Philadel-

especially Dr. Joseph   1779-1840
and his son, Dr. Isaac   1811-1852

phia Board of Health to fill the arduous position of resident physician at the Yellow Fever Hospital. When the need abated he took up general practice. He published articles, gave public lectures on chemistry, served without pay in the Alms House Hospital and the Pennsylvania Hospital, and drew around him a group of students for whose medical training he became responsible. At the age of twenty-nine he married Susanna Cox of Burlington. Their home was happy and hospitable. "The covenant of affection" was never broken.

A sketch by his son, Dr. Isaac, informs us in some detail about his preparation to meet the cholera epidemic of 1832. Dr. Joseph Parrish, he says,

"... was invested with the charge of a hospital in Jones alley. . . . This location was in the immediate vicinity of the place of his birth, and was connected with many of his early recollections; a circumstance which he made use of much to the advantage of his fellow citizens. The Alley was principally occupied by hucksters, some of whom were advanced in years, and had known him from childhood. They were violent in their opposition to the proposed hospital, under an apprehension that the disease was contagious, and that it would be brought into their midst. They remonstrated and threatened. . . . Under these circumstances their old friend went among them, visiting their humble habitations, and endeavoring to calm their fears.

"He soon discovered the leader of the opposition, an old woman of violent passions and of great influence in the Alley. To her he chiefly addressed himself, and by his immediate knowledge of her peculiar disposition, succeeded with admirable tact in silencing her opposition, and even in securing her co-operation in the proposed plan.

"In the various preparations necessary for fitting up the building, he employed the poor women of the Alley, paying them liberal wages, thus familiarizing them with the building and making warm friends of many of them.

"It is remarkable that scarcely a case of the disease occurred in the Alley, although many were brought from the adjoining districts—hence the confidence of the inhabitants in their old and long-tried friend was increased."

As in this instance so throughout his life two secrets of the doctor's success were these: he spared no pains and he understood people. His tongue and pen were devoted to whatever seemed calculated to advance the happiness of mankind. He succeeded Thomas Shipley as president of the Anti-Slavery Society; he protested against capital punishment; he took a deep interest in the plight of the American Indians. And he pleaded against cruelty to animals. He had a faithful horse named Lion, that was known all over Philadelphia. Lion survived his master, who made careful provision for him in his will with explicit instructions such as this: "if his teeth should fail, I desire that soft and nutritious food shall be carefully provided for him." Lion passed a well-cared for old age with the doctor's son, Joseph, at Oxmead, the family farm near Burlington.

Like Dr. Fothergill, Dr. Joseph Parrish

was a devoted and consistent member of the Society of Friends, meticulous in his adherence to Quaker dress, regular in attendance at meetings for worship and business. In the business of the Society he exercised brotherly love, not pressing his own views above those of others. He learned Hebrew and Greek so as to feel closer to the actual wording of the Scriptures. Especially he exhorted the young people with whom he was constantly surrounded "to give reverent heed to the Divine principle of light and life in the soul."

His fund of anecdotes was inexhaustible, and among these none was more remarkable than his attendance in 1832 upon the eccentric statesman, John Randolph of Roanoke, Virginia, descendant of Pocahontas, member of Congress, orator, Minister of the United States to Russia.

When bound, as he had hoped, for Europe, John Randolph was seized with illness on his way to Philadelphia. Called to attend him in a hotel, Dr. Parrish asked how long he had been ill, to which Randolph replied, "From birth." In spite of his condition Randolph proceeded to discuss Quakers. "Complimenting us," says the doctor, "in his peculiar manner for neatness, economy, order, comfort, in everything right, in everything, except politics —there always twistical."

He informed the doctor of his will manumitting his two hundred slaves and providing for their support. Dr. Parrish was informed that the law of Virginia required that a declaration be made in the presence of a white witness, who should thereafter remain with the testator until he was dead; but he was embarrassed to serve alone in this capacity since he was known not to be impartial on the subject of slavery. Locked in the chamber of the dying patient he insisted that other witnesses be called. Only those who know the singular appearance of Randolph of Roanoke can imagine the scene. Propped up by his faith-

ful body servant, John, he rallied all his energies.

"Pointing towards us," records Dr. Parrish, "with his long index finger, he thus addressed us—'I confirm all the directions in my will respecting my slaves, and direct them to be enforced, particularly in regard to a provision for their support,' then raising his arm as high as he could, he brought it down with his open hand on the shoulder of his favorite John, adding these words, 'especially for this man'. . . ."

Soon after this communication he expired. In spite of his busy life Dr. Parrish went to Richmond to testify before the court in charge of the case, and the will was eventually confirmed.

We reproduce the silhouette of John Randolph of Roanoke with his beloved horses in the background, done by William Henry Brown. Concerning this profile of his old political enemy Henry Clay told the artist, "It is the very perfection of your art." And so it is; every line indicates the character of this able, cantankerous, witty old statesman.

As parent of eleven children Dr. Joseph Parrish desired for them a superior and guarded education in the Society of Friends. For this he made provision in his will. He died in 1840 at the age of sixty-one, having his children about him "as olive branches round the table," to quote his biblical expression.

Of the eleven only one died early. The eldest, Dillwyn, who was resident of the College of Pharmacy assisted with the incorporation of the Woman's Medical College. "A body of women students when first admitted to the study of medicine was hooted through the streets of Philadelphia by men students on the sidewalk, the women marching in the middle of the street with Dillwyn Parrish at their head."

Dillwyn's younger brother, Dr. Isaac Parrish, 1811-1852, who appears with his father in our silhouette by August Edouart, was the second son. His name can be seen today inscribed in the vestibule of the College of Physicians in Philadelphia, among those who died in performance of duty during pestilence and during war. Dr. Parrish was stricken by an epidemic disease, perhaps cholera, in the course of attendance upon patients, including his own eldest son who also died.

For twenty years Isaac Parrish had been, not only an active family doctor, but, like his father, an efficient participant in enterprises for the public good, particularly in prison reform. He was one of the founders and contributing editors of the *Friends Intelligencer,* since become the *Friends Journal.* A beloved physician, his early death was mourned not only by his family and colleagues, but by the whole city.

Another brother, Edward, who early in life

wrote an *Introduction to Practical Pharmacy,* many years later became organizer, fund raiser, and finally first president of Swarthmore College. Some forty years afterward Parrish Hall, formerly just called "The College," was named in his honor. The younger Parrishes, daughters as well as sons, were all philanthropists who initiated or took part in the founding of much needed institutions and societies for the care of disadvantaged persons, inebriates, beggars, retarded children, aged and infirm colored people, and others. Such were the remarkable children ·of dedicated and gifted parents.

Joseph Sturge   1793-1859

IN 1853, exhausted by sightseeing in Scotland, the author of *Uncle Tom's Cabin* and her husband, Calvin, reached Birmingham in a drizzle of April rain which made the industrial midlands look more than usually dull and sooty. They were to be met by Joseph Sturge, but wondered how they should recognize him and he them. Calvin ventured out on the station platform to look for their host, as Harriet records:

"Sure enough, in a few moments he pitched upon a cheerful, middle-aged gentleman, with a moderate but not decisive broad brim to his hat, and challenged him as Mr. Sturge; the result verified the truth that 'instinct is a great matter.' In a few moments our new friend and ourselves were snugly encased in a fly, trotting off as briskly as ever we could to his place at Edgbaston. . . . The carriage soon drove in upon a gravel walk, winding among turf, flowers, and shrubs, where we found opening to us another home, warm and kindly. . . . After retiring to our chambers to repair the ravages of travel, we united in the pleasant supper-room, where the table was laid before a bright coal-fire; no unimportant feature this fire, I can assure you, in a raw cloudy evening. A glass-door from the supper room opened into a conservatory, brilliant with pink and yellow azaleas, golden calcelarias, and a profusion of other beauties, whose names I did not know.

"The side tables were strewn with books, and the ample folds of the drab curtains, let down over the windows, shut out the rain, damp, and chill. . . . I must not omit to say that the evening circle was made more attractive and agreeable in my eyes by the presence of two or three of the little people, who were blessed with the rosy cheeks of English children. . . .

"Mr. Sturge is one of the most prominent and efficient of the philanthropists of modern days. An air of benignity and easy good nature veils and conceals in him the most unflinching perseverance and energy of purpose. . . ."

From *Sunny Memories of Foreign Lands*

Joseph Sturge was a wholesale wheat merchant and importer. In this highly speculative enterprise, intimately connected with the food supply of the poor, he continued throughout his life in partnership with his brothers. To the outside world he appeared to be the "ideal Christian merchant." But he knew in his conscience with what difficulties and temptations the wheat trade was attended, and he admitted that it required more "circumspection and watchfulness" than he had sometimes exercised.

He was early convinced that laying up wealth, even for one's children, was not justified, often proving a curse to the younger generation. But he realized that his career of public service was made possible by his independent means. The anti-slavery movement and peace shared "the innermost place in the warm heart of Joseph Sturge," but the concern he felt for British wage-earners was hardly less insistent. The demand for universal suffrage and the need for education drew upon his sympathy. He was active in the then new Adult School movement. The evils in which England was implicated abroad, especially the slave trade, the opium wars in

China, and the extension of the Empire by force of arms in Asia and Africa also drew upon his boundless energy.

It was the anti-slavery cause that first took him from England. The slave trade had been legally abolished by Great Britain in 1807. Twenty-seven years later the slaves in the West Indies were ostensibly freed by purchase, but there was a proviso that they should work seven years longer for their old masters. Joseph Sturge made the hard journey by sailing vessel to the British West Indies to see for himself how the arrangement was working, and he came home to lay before the public and members of Parliament such a series of grim facts as caused the termination in 1838 of the so-called apprenticeship system.

Before his death Joseph Sturge bought a small island in the Caribbean where he hoped to show that sugar could be profitably grown by free labor, but the land was not suited for sugar cane. However, it was found that lime trees could flourish there, and a prosperous colony of Negro landholders developed the production and export of lime juice.

The latter years of life were devoted to the cause of peace. Most familiar to Friends is his mission to Russia to try to persuade the Czar to prevent the Crimean War. England was in such a war fever that Friends there could not influence their own government. With two other Friends he made the winter journey to St. Petersburg by sledge. The Czar received the delegation kindly, but when news reached Russia of inflammatory speeches in the British parliament the negotiations failed.

After the war Joseph Sturge set out for Paris to see what he could do for the Peace Treaty. This time the outcome was more encouraging, for the delegation succeeded in getting a provision binding the signatory powers to submit disputes to arbitration. In the wake of the

Crimean War (1854) Joseph Sturge also explored the damage to the coast of Finland caused by the British navy. This was followed by a British Quaker relief project conducted through a Finnish committee. On the way home Joseph Sturge again visited Russia and talked with the Czar Alexander who succeeded Nicholas whom he had visited earlier.

No wonder the English statesman Cobden wrote to the Secretary of the Peace Society:

> "It is really refreshing to see Sturge's inexhaustible energy. He could run a dozen young men off their legs. No sooner is he back from his visit to Russia than he inquires if there is nothing to be done! I have sometimes wondered what such men would do, if the world's crimes and follies did not find them plenty of employment in the work of well-doing."

All the while, as his wife once wrote, her husband shed abroad in their household a "fragrance of blessing." Some of this happy domesticity is reflected in the two silhouettes reproduced here. The larger hangs in the living room at Pendle Hill, the reduced reproduction shows a replica which I saw several years ago in the home of William Albright of Birmingham, England. The two are very nearly duplicates, the products of a technique whereby a folded sheet of paper is cut to produce at least two identical or almost identical examples of each of the figures in a group. These might then be mounted in the same or a different order on prepared backgrounds. In our two illustrations, though the parents are reversed, the order of the children is the same. It will be noted that the carpet patterns are dissimilar and that the backgrounds differ somewhat in horticultural detail.

The Sturge children totalled four girls and a boy. This gives us the clue by which to date our silhouette in which only three girls appear, the youngest as yet unborn. I would

49

hazard 1853—the year of Harriet Beecher Stowe's visit. The baby shown here in her mother's lap is Lily Sturge (Albright), who wrote the sketch of her father's life for children in America, published in the Second Series of *Quaker Biographies, Volume V.* The Sturge biography for adults is by Stephen Hobhouse, London, 1919, a most readable book, but the old six hundred page *Memoirs,* 1864, by Henry Richard, furnishes the basis of all subsequent accounts.

Though Joseph Sturge did not write a Journal, he published a three hundred page account entitled *A Visit to the United States in 1841.* The chief subjects to claim his attention on this tour were the abolition of slavery and the promotion of permanent international peace. This book written more than one hundred and twenty years ago is informative today in view of the current civil rights crisis. From it the reader can judge how far opinion has moved in the intervening years.

Conclusion

DURING OUR progress from 1750 to 1850 we have encountered many changes. When Dr. Fothergill in the mid-eighteenth century hurried to the bedside of a distant patient his "exceedingly lusty" coachman drove him in a dark green coach drawn by tall black horses; whereas Harriet Beecher Stowe, at her meeting with Joseph Sturge in 1853, arrived by steam. And so thoroughly had the concept of mechanical locomotion captured the spirit of the age that it is reflected in the smokestack of a child's toy train.

As ways of transportation, of communication, and of industrial production changed, so did ways of thinking. It is not suprising that the Society of Friends was stirred to re-examine itself. For beneath the tranquil surface it was a world in conflict. On the one hand the Quakers had become a highly unified group, "very strict and exact" in minor matters. The century 1750-1850 was a period of stressing the discipline, of "conscious conformity to correct method." Could this conformity answer the requirements of the changing world? asked certain concerned members. Awakened consciences answered, "No." It could not. If obedience to the Inward Guide is a living reality it means responding to new, and newly perceived, needs as they arise.

The response was at first individual, then corporate. For as in all times so in this period there were individuals who exhibited unusual initiative, a few who showed the touch of genius. As individuals perceived the grave inconsistency with Christian principles of poverty, war, slave holding, the penal system, and other evils, Quakers had first to convince their own society, then as the conviction spread and arose spontaneously elsewhere, the public at large had to be persuaded. First the evil must be seen, next the remedy sought. The third step is to qualify people for change. Finally the improved condition will be taken for granted.

Our last illustration, a hollow-cut by a certain Miss Glover, inspired by one of the great persuaders of this period, illustrates Matthew 25, "I was in prison and ye came unto me. . . ." Here, pictured in the pre-photographic medium, is Elizabeth Fry. Bonnet in hand, she stands by T. Fowell Buxton, the husband of her sister Hannah, and one of the founders of the "Society for the Reformation of Prison Discipline." At the left a chained prisoner lies on his bed of straw. A turnkey carries two big keys of the period. At the right is a little Quaker girl, possibly one of Elizabeth Fry's eleven children, who accompanied her before the danger from contagious disease was realized.

Because of her poise and dignity Elizabeth Fry often impressed people as being tall. Here she appears small beside her massive brother-in-law, whose school fellows called him "elephant Buxton," he being well over six feet tall, a far more unusual height at the time than it would be today. It requires great skill to produce a hollow-cut, particularly one with such fine detail as is shown here in the straw and the keys, fetters and bonnet string.

This little album *Quaker Profiles,* 1750-1850, has followed the profile process from Patience Wright's medallion of Dr. Fothergill and Sara Hustler's shadow of Rebecca Jones to Edouart's elaborate groups of the Sansoms and Underhills. Finally we conclude with one of the most attractive of Quaker saints at her work with the convicts in Newgate Prison.

Out of this experience Elizabeth Fry wrote in 1831: "Nothing is so likely to cause our Society to remain a living and spiritual body, as its being willing *to stand open to improvement,* . . . My belief is, that neither individuals nor collective bodies should *stand still* in grace, but that their light should shine brighter and brighter unto the perfect day."

A Few Books on Silhouettes

BOSTON, ETHEL STANWOOD. *Wax Portraits and Silhouettes,* Massachusetts Society of Colonial Dames, Boston, 1914.

GARRICK, ALICE VAN LEER. *Shades of Our Ancestors.* Boston, 1928.

JACKSON, MRS. E. NEVILL. *Ancestors in Silhouettes Cut by August Edouart.* London, 1921.

————. *Catalogue of 3,800 Named and Dated American Silhouette Portraits by August Edouart.* London, 192—.

————. *Silhouette, Notes and Dictionary.* London, 1938.

LISTER, RAYMOND. *Silhouettes, an Introduction to Their History and to the Art of Cutting and Painting Them.* London, 1952.

SIMS, LEONARD A. *The Art of Silhouette Cutting.* Foreword by Mrs. E. Nevill Jackson. London, 1937.

VARNEY, ARTHUR S. *A Catalogue of Silhouettes by August Edouart.* Privately printed. New York, 1913.

Periodicals frequently contain articles on silhouettes, especially *The Connoisseur,* London, and *The Craftsman,* New York. To the author's knowledge there has been no published work on Quaker silhouettes as such, except for her own brief, prefatory article, "Quaker Profiles," in *Bulletin of the Friends' Historical Association,* Vol. XXIX, No. 1 (1940), and the recently published article by Charles Coleman Sellers, "Joseph Sansom, Philadelphia Silhouettist," in *The Pennsylvania Magazine,* Vol. LXXXVIII, No. 4 (October, 1964).